Walk the Talk on Hot Coals

By Peter Koren

2025 Edition

ISBN: 978-1-0670654-0-9

Copyright Feb 2017, 2025

Paperback

Published by GLOWING LIGHT LTD
Auckland New Zealand

All rights reserved worldwide.
No part of this publication may be replicated, redistributed, or given away in any form without the prior written consent of the author/publisher or the terms relayed to you herein.

The 2025 Edition has an upgraded cover with no other significant changes.
The Publisher is GLOWING LIGHT LTD.

Table of Contents

Table of Contents 2
Chapter 1 3
Chapter 2 25
Chapter 3 35
Chapter 4 41
Chapter 5 45
Chapter 6 55
Chapter 7 61
Chapter 8 67
Chapter 9 75
Chapter 10 83

Chapter 1

You've heard of hot coal walking, but what happens when a hot coal is put in your mouth?
Eeks that's gotta hurt! The hot coal goes onto your very sensitive and fragile tongue, what is the reaction?

We know walking on hot coals can be like a fired up party trick that initiates the thrill seeker, or like the extreme living star looking to notch up some high flying stunt; but, not in this case, no, we are talking about something completely unexpected that could happen to you and me!
So, getting back to our story, how would a hot coal effect a person's speech after it got into their mouth and then it did things to their tongue?

Well that's exactly what happened to a celebrated prophet of God named Isaiah and his experience is the focus of this novel.
Isaiah was taken into Heaven, into the very throne room of God and beheld His Presence and Majesty and to say the least, he was awe struck by this mind shattering event.
How would you feel being in the presence of the creator of the universe and standing before the presence of a perfect and all knowing God?

Not something us mortals usually face in our life times, as far as I know, very few have been there. So how did Isaiah handle it? He was devastated and he cried out *"woe is me I am a man of unclean lips."*

After Isaiah collapsed from the initial shock of this encounter, a Seraphim *(Angel)* from the throne room of God brought a hot coal and placed it into Isaiah's mouth and it definitely got Isaiah's tongue.

Why a hot coal in the mouth?
Why not place Isaiah on the challenge to walk on hot coals to see if he is worthy?
Gods ways are higher than our ways! Isaiah 55.
Obviously the effect of the hot coal into the mouth was way different to a person deciding to take up the challenge and walk the hot coals.

Although, when the hot coal walker does this trick it could be something related to spiritual activity happening, elevating the walker somehow.
Let's face it, we are all searching for the ultimate and some experiences may take us higher up to the mountain top.

God knows how we tick and He has the walk that can get us to our destination. He has something far reaching and life changing than a trip to find ourselves on our way to Shangri-La La.

Isaiah became undone in the presence of the Almighty God and who wouldn't be undone? Then to help Isaiah compose himself, he got the hot coal treatment, what happened to bliss?

Keep in mind this is a chosen prophet of God, someone that was specifically chosen to be brought into Heaven, into God's Throne room for a specific purpose.
Isaiah was someone who was seeking God in intense prayer, devoted to serving the plans and intentions of God for his life, Isaiah was submitted to God's will being done, desiring to be and do all that God had planned for his life.

God sure has a way of working out Isaiah's ability to stand up and be strong, to endure this encounter. Although this heavenly visit initially devastated Isaiah to his very core, it is apparent that in God's wisdom, this is what Isaiah needed to change him forever and prepare him for what was to come.
Isaiah, like any of us was subject to the effects of iniquity, which is worked into our very DNA from birth, as King David declared, *"I was born into iniquity". Psalm 51.*

Iniquity is the tendency to go off on crooked tangents with repeated undesirable thinking and destructive choices, which is reinforcing like a triggered, malicious program to execute in our lives. This pattern of iniquity works into our beings from previous generations of bad choices and will try to influence us into the same old negatives!

We don't always choose the right pill, or maybe we do choose the right pill and say why did I choose that pill? I should have stayed in the land of bliss doing my own thing, no worries, just the good life and hell, why not walk on hot coals, where is the harm in that?

This might be a blissful moment, but as it is said, *"you gotta serve somebody," Bob Dylan.*

There is no neutral ground, a free fire state, we all got to choose one way or another!

Or, better put, we choose one Kingdom that is put inside us, or we choose the other one, where we are misled into thinking we are above it all! One is right and in the light and the other is well, on a track that makes us look like a bright spark, but is a trip into the black hole.

Isaiah 6
7"Behold, this has touched your lips;
Your iniquity is taken away,
And your sin purged."
8 Also I heard the voice of the Lord, saying:
"Whom shall I send,
And who will go for Us?"
Then I said, "Here am I! Send me."
9 And He said, "Go, and tell this people……….."
The question is asked who is going to tell the nations about the state they are in and the way to be saved from our mess?

The changes to Isaiah's inner being and his soul was profound.
Isaiah became a prophet and a spokesman to the people of God and the nations, he shook the earth with the messages he brought and prophesized future world changing events, as well as prophesying the coming of Jesus the Saviour of this world. Isaiah's words and declarations brought the powers of Heaven and Gods will into the earth.

Isaiah was a gifted and very articulate prophet and his messages were pure poetry as well as being the voice that represented Heaven.

Now I must mention we aren't a carbon copy of Isaiah, we won't get the same fire treatment or experience in heaven like he did, each one is unique and how God moves and each one's life is different, but still out of this world.

Having a religious experience is not what this book is about primarily, it is more about how God moves in our lives to bring purity into our beings that will change us forever and set our paths and the things that we say and do on the right course.
Our history has happened to us, but our future is open for change and all sorts of possibilities.
It isn't about being like the hot coal walkers wild experience and getting a hell of a hot kick out of life; you know it may burn your toes off if you are not careful with what you get into.
Sorry to the walkers, but there is a lot more to this than can be seen with the natural eye and there are deeper things that can bring us into our true identity and to be a true voice for our times and place.

Isaiah 49:1-2
"Listen, O coastlands, to Me,
And take heed, you peoples from afar!
The LORD has called Me from the womb;
From the matrix of My mother He has made mention of My name.
2 And He has made My mouth like a sharp sword;
In the shadow of His hand He has hidden Me,
And made Me a polished shaft;
In His quiver He has hidden Me."

The human capacity is destined for great and powerful things; much is being pursued and developed by those wanting to take the human potential where it hasn't been before.
Our imagination powers can take the mind into the galaxies, maybe we might even gain super powers like Generation X Y and Z men
Well, God has taken the hot coal walking experience which is pretty far out and on the fringe, which looks pretty impressive by our standards and taken it to a whole new other level.
Think fired up like never before

Hot Coal Walking is a wild practice which is considered to elevate our abilities.
Hold on! You might object to this practice as questionable, but I am just referring to this as an illustration to apply a spiritual meaning, not really recommending burning your feet, tempting fate, or challenging the gods or whatever.
Black magic does exist. No doubt! But let's focus on what is good and even miraculous.

Consider this, even Jesus as a man on earth was dependant on the goodness of God.
Mark 10:18 New King James Version (NKJV)
18 So Jesus said to him, "Why do you call Me good? No one is good but One, that is, God.

We won't go too deep here, but as one who went before us, so that we could walk the talk like He did, the Word of God became Immanuel, God with us. He is the light of the world and the light that lights us up, He became a man in order that we could follow Him and be conformed to His image resulting from the sacrifice He made on the cross.

This is very interesting to be aware of as Jesus Himself as a man declared His dependence on God the Father, Jesus was sinless and He still depended on God for His life.

So much more any man or woman needs to be connected to the Father and not be a roaming, free agent, firing wild cannon shots at the world as a supposed authority and agent to fix things, how we see fit.

Philippians 2:7- 9 New King James Version (NKJV)
7 but made Himself of no reputation, taking the form of a bondservant, and coming in the likeness of men.
8 And being found in appearance as a man, He humbled Himself and became obedient to the point of death, even the death of the cross.
9 Therefore God also has highly exalted Him and given Him the name which is above every name,

Getting back to the coal walkers, the principle is here and the same can be flipped into the positive. *Doug Addison* phrase - "flip it and flip it good".

The walkers need some kind of power to get them across without burning them, by natural laws they would be burnt, when they walked on the burning hot coals. As believers we are able to walk across trials and testings of fire, we are cleansed by the power of the blood of Jesus and so, we receive a higher power from the Man from Heaven, without this power we would burn unless we turn, no cross and we can't get across.

What is across and where does it take us? First of all we are translated out of the Kingdom of darkness into the Kingdom of His light and we have crossed over from slavery and the dominion of darkness into the promises of God by a journey of faith.

This doesn't mean that we don't have baggage anymore when we receive salvation, it means that the baggage is burnt up as we go through the trials and testings and allow God to refine our faith.

Heb 10
14 For by one offering He has perfected forever those who are being sanctified.

The sacrifice of Jesus gets us in the door, but we still need to walk across into the promises of the higher life and that is a faith exercise and there is testing fires and hot coals that can burn our walk if we don't apply faith.

We walk by faith and not by sight. 2 Corinthians 5:7

Best to look up and not look down where the hot burning coals are right under our feet. Look to the destination and not at the fiery obstacles that are in front of us.

By faith and patience we inherit the promises. Hebrews 6:12

James 1:3,4
3 knowing that the testing of your faith produces patience.
4 But let patience have its perfect work, that you may be perfect and complete, lacking nothing.

We still need to enter into a process of refinement and each step of the way means we are dependant on Him to progress to the other side where the promises are obtained.

There are things that will weigh us down, baggage that slows us up, distractions from making it across in good time. There are pitfalls that can trip us or make us fall and we need to turn our eyes upon Jesus, who is our example and forerunner, showing us the way to walk above the natural elements.

Let's continue by seeing how this refinement as a hot coal treatment, was applied to a highly esteemed prophet of God.

Isaiah 6
6 Then one of the seraphim flew to me, having in his hand a live coal which he had taken with the tongs from the altar.
7 And he touched my mouth with it, and said:
"Behold, this has touched your lips;
Your iniquity is taken away,
And your sin purged."

Isaiah experienced a dramatic heavenly vision of the Glory of the Lord in the Glorious Throne Room of Heaven.
"Woe is me he cried, I am a man of unclean lips living with a people of unclean lips"
What a reaction you would think a heavenly experience as significant as that would utterly astound him and bring him delight beyond measure.

Something he could broadcast to the world about seeing the splendors of a Heavenly experience and a life changing encounter.
No doubt he was overwhelmed and this experience would change him forever and he was chosen to be a witness to the Glory of God in Heaven.
This encounter was for a reason as well as part of the calling Isaiah had as a prophet, to take the message of God and publish it.

The presence of God and the power of the Glory in Heaven is beyond anything that we normally experience on earth in our natural realm, the attributes of Gods Holy perfection will contrast with our fallen nature and human carnal state.
This will bring anyone to their knees.

However, it is Gods will to bring His Glory to us and fill the whole earth.

His presence is everywhere even if we are not aware of it and He wants us to experience this in our daily walk, also it is possible that to experience Heaven may be granted as well.

But we are people with unclean lips, who can speak life and also death cannot stand in His presence without this condition being dealt with, when we come to the realisation of who He is and the Glory that He is, we are undone in His presence, by sheer perfect light and power that is of a super higher energy and frequency, that is way beyond what natural man can endure. Similar to voltage, as something we can identify with, in other words a bit like those high voltage power lines that are extremely dangerous to touch.

Also, His brilliance of pure high energy light in its complete splendor, just obliterates the darkness in us.

God the Father is gracious and full of compassion, so in His great mercy, sent an angel with a hot coal from His alter and this was applied to Isaiah's lips, causing him to be cleansed of impurities in his speaking, so that he could stand in the presence of God. Not only was Isaiah in this great Glory, but he could see Him and hear Him speak without being obliterated.

Know that what is in our hearts, this is what comes out as we speak from our inner man the soul, it is from the nature of our beings where we draw our life from. How we respond to life situations comes from this inner well of our value systems and memories, it could be bad or it could be good, the true intent and motivations will become apparent.

God is asking who can He send to bring a message to men on earth?
You know this message that God wants to bring to mankind must be spoken by a man or woman who has the words of God written or spoken into his or her heart.
Because Isaiah received a cleansing refinement to his speech and he was called as a
prophet by God, he was now able to respond *"send me"*.

Isaiah can now look into the Glory of God and hear what He is saying without the clamor of darkness in his heart and the contamination of unclean lips.

You see a transformation took place in Isaiah from being completely undone in Gods presence, to being a messenger of Gods Glory and His words of life to the nations.
This is also about Isaiah's calling to be a prophet and fulfilling what was already written about him on a scroll in heaven.

Psalm 40
6 Sacrifice and offering You did not desire;
My ears You have opened.
Burnt offering and sin offering You did not require.
7 Then I said, "Behold, I come;
In the scroll of the book it is written of me.
8 I delight to do Your will, O my God,
And Your law is within my heart."
This passage was about the coming Messiah who is Jesus and He was sent before us as firstfruits of the resurrection power of God that qualifies us, to be His messengers on earth.

We all have our own unique voice on earth, a message, a role, an expression that is our unique foot print, however we all need to enter into the process of refinement and this begins by salvation through the door of Jesus the Saviour of the world, followed by a life walk to be more like Him.
Bob Jones heard when he visited heaven *"did you learn to love?"*

Yes we are still imperfect this side of His return to earth, but He has cleansed us by His Word and commissioned us to go forth and carry the glory into the whole earth, *as He is so are we in the world. 1 John*

Now the odd thing here is Isaiah just came into a heavenly experience that would radically change anyone and in this experience God cleansed him and made him capable to stand in such Glory.
Yet we find that he is given a message to tell the people that they are dull of hearing the things of God and cannot see the Glory of God.

Where does that leave us?

What happens now when we walk on hot coals?
Now I am not suggesting you get into a hocus pocus party trick and defy the laws of common sense to walk on hot burning coals.

See it like the walk in the spirit and you wont fulfill the lusts of the flesh (Gal 5), lifestyle and this will clear your mind as to what this means symbolically.

You see we are deaf and we are blind until we experience what I might call a hot coal experience, yes Isaiah did see and hear before he got the hot coal refinement, but he was undone by what he saw and heard until the hot coal cleansed him, now he could endure the Glory of God and go out and do what he was assigned to do from birth and be a voice of God.

We are in the same boat, if you put hot coals under a wooden boat it will burn it to bits or at least put a hole in it and it will sink.

Jesus declared *"you are cleansed by the word I have spoken"*, the disciples were now qualified by the Authority and the cleansing power that Jesus has given to them, which applies to us as well. We can now experience the Glory of God and then be commissioned to do what we were born to do on this earth. The Glory of God has filled this earth, but can we see it and can we hear what He is saying?

He who knew no sin became sin for us so that we could be the righteousness of God.
2 Corinthians 5:21
Once we accept Jesus as our Lord and Saviour, we are now qualified and cleansed which means we have the righteousness of God and we are no longer undone, this is our position of grace provided by God when we come into contact with His Glory.
This is the perfect will of our Loving Heavenly Father to redeem us back into a relationship with Him as sons and daughters bearing His DNA, His Glory, His Image, His likeness so we can truly represent Him on earth being carriers of His Glory and Grace, bringing Good News to the earth.

By grace we are saved and this is not due to our own works, so that no man can say I did it without help from God and became like Him. That would be arrogance
However, this is the step into the position of grace where we are able to receive from God and then walk into His blessings by faith, allowing His process to refine us to grow and develop into our potential in Him.

Thankfully, this connection that we make with God the Father is like an entry point, otherwise if we were faced with the Glory of God we would not be able to stand and become completely ruined in His pure presence and we would feel totally inadequate, unqualified, unworthy by the weight of the Glory of God overwhelming us to the point that our unrighteousness would destroy us in His presence.

God is full of grace and mercy and that is not His will for us that we would be destroyed, rather His will is that we all can experience renewal and come freely into His presence to receive love, acceptance, directions, instructions, favour, commissioning and all that He has planned for our lives.

Now Isaiah would not have come into this throne room encounter with God without some preparation I believe. So, we also will not be brought into a powerful encounter with God too quickly, until in the wisdom of God He has prepared a plan for us to endure it. I believe that we do enter into an eternal process of being changed from glory to glory by faith in a continued and abiding relationship with Him.

Many believers including myself who are qualified by the blood of Jesus struggle to hear God clearly, let alone have visions and heavenly encounters and wonder is this all there is to having the born again experience!

What stops us from entering into heavenly encounters with the Lord?

The pure in heart will see God. Matthew 5:8

Psalm 139
23 Search me, O God, and know my heart: try me, and know my thoughts:
24 And see if there be any wicked way in me, and lead me in the way everlasting.

Most of us who have a passion to progress in our faith are hungry to experience the Glory of God.

Don't be discouraged, keep going before Him and put first the Kingdom of God and His Righteousness and He will draw near to you as you draw near to Him and give you His best for your life.

He knows the timing and all of your days are recorded in His book.

Psalm 139
14 I will praise thee; for I am fearfully and wonderfully made: marvelous are thy works; and that my soul knoweth right well.
15 My substance was not hid from thee, when I was made in secret, and curiously wrought in the lowest parts of the earth.
16 Thine eyes did see my substance, yet being imperfect; and in thy book all my members were written, which in continuance were fashioned, when as yet there was none of them.
17 How precious also are thy thoughts unto me, O God! how great is the sum of them!

18 If I should count them, they are more in number than the sand: when I awake, I am still with thee.

If there is anything hidden or blocking your way? He will reveal it and open it up so that you can find His liberty and freedom in His presence.

Isaiah was cleansed in this encounter, but also notice there is a reference to **iniquity** being taken away. *Your iniquity is taken away.*
This taken away and dealings is an action taking place, to remove something that is lodged or embedded, connected to associations or mindsets and it could refer to a behaviour pattern that is programmed into the soul.

In order for the Lord to work this in Isaiah's life there would have been a preparation time for his interaction with the Lord, getting to know Him and His ways and making adjustments into his thinking to align with *Gods ways, which are higher than our ways. Isaiah 55*
This process would have prepared Isaiah for this encounter with the Lord to enable an easy letting go of his flawed carnal characteristics embedded into his soul; which would be the crooked ways which leads to perverse lips or speech.
It is important what words we speak, words have power and life in them to create, to frame our future, or to tear down and harm our life or the lives of others spoken against.

The Lord treats what we say very seriously, as it has power to affect for the better or for the worse. Death and life are in the tongue, blessing and cursing are in our speech.

Crooked ways are made straight - Isaiah 45:2

All we need to do then is engage with the Lord on a regular basis in a lifestyle pursuit of His ways which are higher than our ways and to rearrange our thoughts to align with Gods thoughts which are higher than ours

Romans 12:1,2
I beseech you therefore, brethren, by the mercies of God, that you present your bodies a living sacrifice, holy, acceptable to God, which is your reasonable service.
2 And do not be conformed to this world, but be transformed by the renewing of your mind, that you may prove what is that good and acceptable and perfect will of God.

Offering our bodies and allowing the renewing of our mind is a process that we are expected to enter into, as stewards of the gifts that we are given and our own right of free choice to see God and His Glory enter into our beings and life.

His Glory fills the earth and it is available to all who desire the higher life, we can have increase by entering into His plan and refinement to be conformed to the image of Christ.

I have felt very distant and removed from the experiences of God at times in my spiritual journey, but I am encouraged to continue to pursue the higher ways and calling and forget what is behind, pressing into what He has prepared for me to be and do.

Let God into our souls, allowing Him to work His ways into the make up of our character, we enter into the process willingly which allows a renewal of our thinking, which lifts us up to seeing and hearing His ways which are higher than our carnal ways.

The removal of iniquity is more like reprogramming bad habit patterns that are lodged into our character, allowing us to be changed into His likeness.

We need this renewal before we can actually see Him or hear what He is saying clearly.

Otherwise, what we see and hear becomes filtered by the fog of iniquity which is distorted by unwanted impurities and dross which tarnish the pure gold from shining its lustre.

Isaiah 6
10 "Make the heart of this people dull,
And their ears heavy,
And shut their eyes;
Lest they see with their eyes,
And hear with their ears,
And understand with their heart,
And return and be healed."

When our iniquity is removed we will see with our eyes enlightened and hear with our ears opened by the Spirit of God.

We will be changed into His likeness to understand with our hearts, His ways which are higher than our ways.

Isaiah 29:13 New King James Version (NKJV)
13 Therefore the Lord said:
"Inasmuch as these people draw near with their mouths
And honor Me with their lips,
But have removed their hearts far from Me,
And their fear toward Me is taught by the commandment of men,

Colossians 2
19 and not holding fast to the Head, from whom all the body, nourished and knit together by joints and ligaments, grows with the increase that is from God.
20 Therefore, if you died with Christ from the basic principles of the world, why, as though living in the world, do you subject yourselves to regulations—
21 "Do not touch, do not taste, do not handle,"
22 which all concern things which perish with the using—according to the commandments and doctrines of men?
23 These things indeed have an appearance of wisdom in self-imposed religion, false humility, and neglect of the body, but are of no value against the indulgence of the flesh.

When we depart from the ways of the Lord or the higher ways by attempting to self impose our own righteousness to measure up to His perfect ways without engagement with Him, these become the independent religious ways that are rules made by man.

Disconnection from the Head is a major problem, as we are now acting independently without any need for God in our lives and no longer receiving the light of life force from Jesus our great Shepherd and overseer of our souls.

We are taking on a form of godliness and practices, but they have no everlasting value and have no power to change the heart to be conformed to His image.
We are Created in Christ Jesus as His workmanship for good works which we are destined to walk in - Eph 2:10

The process will ensure that our call will be effective with everlasting results for each of us and this is to know Him in a relationship based religion and not a rules, based religion built on the commandments of men.
Why cant commandments help us? The law is perfect.

Commandments on their own when we are faced with them without engaging Him such as Isaiah with hot coal applied to his lips, will make us aware of our weaknesses without the Lord changing us from within, we will either run away or try to put on a superficial appearance of good works in pride of what we can do. Only the Lord knows our hearts and minds, only He knows what each day He purposed for us to engage Him and allow His process of change to be more like Him and open the eyes of our understanding and open our ears to hear His instruction, guiding us each day.
Only God knows where we need the change most at any given time, as we can have blind spots to our faults and where we are up to on this journey, towards the higher ways.

Also, if we are condemned then this only creates shame in our hearts which will drive us away from our loving Heavenly Father. We may feel it is hopeless as there is always one vice, one besetting sin that trips us up, where we just can't seem to break the chains.

We are invited onto the Highway of Holiness, where we separated to the Lord, part of His household as sons and daughters, kings and priests in His Kingdom moving forward onwards and upwards from Glory to Glory.

There is a Glory train lets hop aboard for the ride of our life.
If we try to fix our issues ourselves, or follow another man or look to man for answers and ways to self improve, it wont be in accordance with our unique journey, what worked for them will not fit us effectively by the Hand of the Master Craftsman, because, we all have our own unique idiosyncrasies and only the Lord knows how to adjust and tune in harmony.

Discipline is good and following rules is necessary, as long as they are aligned with the Head who is Jesus, He is the Head and we are the Body, we need the connection and to be under the Lordship of Jesus finely tuned, for our unique greatness.

My memories of when I first studied the commandments of God were mixed, the ones that I messed up on I felt like a failure and carried guilt and the more I tried to do them, the more I knew that I was no good at them, comparatively the laws I was good at usually made me look at others that were unable to keep them with a superior look, thinking *"get your act together you heathens"*.

Chapter 2

CD Writer

CD Writer can mean Completely Delivered Writer. Rewritable CDs gives us the ability to rewrite errors and past history.
The laser beam etches out the old data and rewrites brand new data creating a disc that has meaning and purpose, a beautiful correction kept and played at will.

He is the Light of mankind that lights up every man and every woman that allows His Light to rewrite the new creation that Father God's eyes see, which is the identity He imagined we would have.
Jesus has made us His workmanship, admired, uniquely designed, incomparable like the snow flakes, all intricately woven and patterned by the master creator like no other.

"How long?
How long before I see results? Promises that are faded hopes and dreams?"
Remember the caterpillar.
All the caterpillar does is move around crawling across the leaves eating all the good nutrients along the pathway.

Each day the caterpillar looks the same.
A funny looking long worm type of eating machine, creature.
Then one day it stops.

"I need a cocoon some protection, something going on inside, cant explain just follow the instincts and create this protective woven coat and go to sleep, go into a dream."

Colossians 3 New King James Version (NKJV)
If then you were raised with Christ, seek those things which are above, where Christ is, sitting at the right hand of God.
2 Set your mind on things above, not on things on the earth.
3 For you died, and your life is hidden with Christ in God.
4 When Christ who is our life appears, then you also will appear with Him in glory.

When we are hidden and it seems like we are forgotten, this is a time when development happens internally, the hidden man is growing stronger and will be expressed in the seen world when ready.
Inside the chrysalis is an amazing development stage from the caterpillar and that is when the changes really begin and birthing, growth happens for the final destiny, to be a butterfly.

The caterpillar is going through metamorphosis, what does he feel?
"Well what do you know, I feel different, I have more limbs with more abilities that I sense, I feel that I have extended gifts. I can kind of see them, feel them, but I just need to break out."
Breakthrough is required to get us into the promised land of flight and freedom.
This is going to take energy, a drive, a push, determination, I see darkness and webs and holding patterns, but I just got to break through.

One day all things are new - there is a butterfly creature which once was a creepy crawly caterpillar.
"I am free.
I have these powers and abilities I have never known before, feels good, feels fine and feels free.
Now what do I do with this? I am all stiff and stuck.
Just start moving.
Yes there it comes, what do we have here, these are flying wings.
What do I do?
Lets try flip flap flop.
Takes a bit of time, but well wouldn't you know it, I am off the ground.
But how do I control this? I am going to crash, man that was close.
Getting better, a lot better all the time. Whoops that sounds a bit like a
Beatles song, that's OK that works.
I can fly.
I am a new creation."

The process; lets just keep believing, stay in the faith, positioned to fly.
It is written in the DNA of the caterpillar - one day you are a butterfly.
Have you ever seen the Monarch Butterfly?
Magnificent creature full of beauty and freedom, to think it started off as a crawling caterpillar just blows my mind.
We are made a brand new creation.
Jesus is the light of the world.- John 1
His perfect light rewrites our disc. CD - Completely Delivered.
CDs are written using laser beams, which are a powerful light source that is able to lay tracks of information and expression.

A rewrite is possible and new tracks are created.
Jesus is rewriting our tracks.
This is a process, but the end result is marvelous to our eyes.
1 Corinthians 2:9-10 New King James Version (NKJV)
9 But as it is written:
"Eye has not seen, nor ear heard,
Nor have entered into the heart of man
The things which God has prepared for those who love Him."
10 But God has revealed them to us through His Spirit. For the Spirit searches all things, yes, the deep things of God.

Who the Son sets free is free indeed. John 8:36
CD Written.
Hebrews 10:16 New King James Version (NKJV)
16 "This is the covenant that I will make with them after those days, says the Lord: I will put My laws into their hearts, and in their minds I will write them,"

His Glory Light Rewrites us anew.
Lets walk in the light as He is in the Light. 1 John 1:7
Find your Complete Deliverance Today in His Light.
James 3
5 Even so the tongue is a little member and boasts great things.
See how great a forest a little fire kindles!
6 And the tongue is a fire, a world of iniquity.
The tongue is so set among our members that it defiles the whole body, and sets on fire the course of nature; and it is set on fire by hell.
7 For every kind of beast and bird, of reptile and creature of the sea, is tamed and has been tamed by mankind.

8 But no man can tame the tongue. It is an unruly evil, full of deadly poison.
9 With it we bless our God and Father, and with it we curse men, who have been made in the similitude of God.
10 Out of the same mouth proceed blessing and cursing. My brethren, these things ought not to be so.
11 Does a spring send forth fresh water and bitter from the same opening?
12 Can a fig tree, my brethren, bear olives, or a grapevine bear figs? Thus no spring yields both salt water and fresh.

It gets back to what comes out of our mouths, our speech being defiled.

Grumbling, complaining, judging and harsh words, lack of gratitude.

Then there is doubts, fears and unbelief and all of these things have power to bring destruction to our lives and the lives of others affected.

Isaiah 6
11 Then I said, "Lord, how long?"
And He answered:
"Until the cities are laid waste and without inhabitant,
The houses are without a man,
The land is utterly desolate,
12 The Lord has removed men far away,
And the forsaken places are many in the midst of the land.
13 But yet a tenth will be in it,
And will return and be for consuming,
As a terebinth tree or as an oak,
Whose stump remains when it is cut down.
So the holy seed shall be its stump."

He asks how long does it take?
We ask how long is it going to take?

Notice the tree had to be removed and it is the stump where the Holy Seed is and grows.
What is the tree?

It is all that has grown up in our lives creating crooked ways that block our ability to see and hear what God wants and what is best for us, as well as twisting what we are created to be and do on earth.
The iniquity removed leaving just the stump, creates like a fresh slate to write His laws and ways into our hearts and minds anew.
Then it flourishes with nothing choking the life out of it, what is planted, the seeds of righteousness will sprout and grow into a new fruitful righteous tree.

There is much teaching on healing of the soul, gifts of healings, healing of memories, generational curses and removal.
We need to place ourselves in the position of change that we have been freely given by the new birth of salvation and what the freedom offered, by the eternal sacrifice of the Great Shepherd of our souls.
Accept the word with meekness that will save our soul. James 1:21
Pray in the spirit as much as possible, read the word, meditate and assimilate the word, allow the mind of Christ to overlay our thinking to be renewed.
Find His pleasing, acceptable and perfect will
Be in a place of worship, draw near to Him in fellowship and be transformed by His sweet and encompassing presence.
Fasting and Prayer will accelerate the process to remove the blockages to our faith.
2 Corinthians 4:7 we are treasures in clay vessels.
Even if we are cracked pots at times He is still working in us His will and good pleasure.

Walk in the spirit and we won't fulfill the lusts of the flesh. *Gal 5*

Sow to the spirit and we will reap a harvest of His goodness and be pure in heart and see what the Father is doing.

James 3:14-18
14 But if you have bitter envy and self-seeking in your hearts, do not boast and lie against the truth.
15 This wisdom does not descend from above, but is earthly, sensual, demonic.
16 For where envy and self-seeking exist, confusion and every evil thing are there.
17 But the wisdom that is from above is first pure, then peaceable, gentle, willing to yield, full of mercy and good fruits, without partiality and without hypocrisy.
18 Now the fruit of righteousness is sown in peace by those who make peace.

Notice that the wisdom from above is pure, so the pure in heart see God and receive His wisdom and there is no striving and contention to achieve in life, but in a state of peace, the pure in heart appropriate the blessings of God.

The pure is like gold, a refining process has occurred to remove all of the impurities, making fine gold that is valuable and profitable.
Double mindedness is where we are torn between serving the Lord, or serving our selfish desires.

James 4

Where do wars and fights come from among you? Do they not come from your desires for pleasure that war in your members?

2 You lust and do not have. You murder and covet and cannot obtain. You fight and war. Yet you do not have because you do not ask.

3 You ask and do not receive, because you ask amiss, that you may spend it on your pleasures.

4 Adulterers and adulteresses! Do you not know that friendship with the world is enmity with God? Whoever therefore wants to be a friend of the world makes himself an enemy of God.

5 Or do you think that the Scripture says in vain, "The Spirit who dwells in us yearns jealously"?

6 But He gives more grace. Therefore He says:
"God resists the proud,
But gives grace to the humble."

7 Therefore submit to God. Resist the devil and he will flee from you.

8 Draw near to God and He will draw near to you. Cleanse your hands, you sinners; and purify your hearts, you double-minded.

9 Lament and mourn and weep! Let your laughter be turned to mourning and your joy to gloom.

10 Humble yourselves in the sight of the Lord, and He will lift you up.

It all gets back to submitting ourselves to God, if Jesus needed to depend on God for life and goodness and He was a sinless man how much more do we, with all of our sins and iniquities? This is being humble, allowing God's greatness to burn into our weaknesses, through the resurrection ability and the life of Jesus.

2 Corinthians 3:18
But we all, with unveiled face, beholding as in a mirror the glory of the Lord, are being transformed into the same image from glory to glory, just as by the Spirit of the Lord.

May we experience this process of pure change in His presence, as we approach Him by the grace provided by Jesus in order that we may become more like Him.

Chapter 3

The Times

The Glory is intensifying.
Many will have a hot coal experience to take them into the Glory of God like never before.

Just remember it is *Not by Might Not by Power but By My Spirit says the Lord.*
The mountain will be removed with shouts of *"Grace, Grace to it."*
More grace I say bring it on.

The systems and principalities of this world that keep our hearts and minds blind to the truth of Gods intense Glory is being shaken and will fall.

Remember that fire has purifying and refining powers to cleanse us from impurities and the waste products in the dross.

Gold and Silver is refined this way in intense heat to draw out the waste and the mixtures to get the pure. However, we couldn't take all of that heat at once, so by the mercies of God there is a manageable process that removes these impurities to refine us and make better you-s and better me-s.

There is a refinement process of what belongs to the Lord on the earth being established.

The Lord says, "the Gold and Silver are Mine".

"What is pure and precious belongs to Me and originated with Me.
Know that without My creation of the characteristics and properties of gold and silver they would not exist.

What is expressed by the characteristics of gold and silver today in creation come from
Me and they can be used or misused however intended by the user.
The elements are subject to mankind and what was originally created in purity can be corrupted on earth. This is where dishonest scales and measures can bring corruption to what is intended to be pure.

This day the purity of gold and silver will be expressed as I have intended from a heart that is surrendered and submitted to My will being done on earth as it is in Heaven.
You will see misappropriated wealth and riches transferred into My plans and purposes established by My vessels of honour and purity refined like gold and silver.
Your faith although going through testing and hardships will go through the refining fires of My Spirit to be purified and shining in the Glory of the Lord. The Church is under the Head who is the King of kings and is a chosen royal priesthood.

My representatives on earth will be directed by the Mind of Christ and be a people after the Heart of the Father, as they are refined, molded and made pliable in the image of Christ, they will become pure in their motives and precious to be like gold and silver vessels who reflect the Glory of Heaven.

The pure in heart will see God move in their lives, in their families, in their communities, in their nation and throughout the earth in each designated sphere of influence, spreading like the wildfire from Heaven and they will say this is supernatural it can't be like this, we have never known so much love expressed and miracles poured out unless Heaven is now working on earth".

Gold qualities are that it is a soft metal and very pliable and can spread very thin.
Resistant to most acids, very sought after and is a precious metal and a very good conductor, with good resistance to corrosion.
Silver is the best metal conductor of heat and electricity known, pliable and can endure heat. Silver is also able to reflect light very well. Also, silver has healing and cleansing properties.

Apply these properties to the body of Christ and you have a very powerful, sought out and effective people. In Him we will be excellent conductors for the anointing of the Holy Spirit, very pliable and willing to move with His leading, resistant to corruption, withstanding heat and pressure, reflecting His light in purity and a carrier of His healing power, this is what the world needs now.

Differences between counterfeit and genuine is hard to detect by the untrained eye and only those by constant use and experience will spot the difference readily.

The Gold and Silver coin market offers a highly desirable product which holds lasting value and makes for a secure investment.

However, unscrupulous thieves are copying and making fake versions of these quality originals.

The Gold and Silver coin market has been bombarded by these fakes which are pretty clever copies using modern technology and because of the great market price for bullion, the cunning crooks are raking in illegal profits.

They have even made gold and silver bars by filling the interior with lead and other mixtures of metals other than the genuine, to deceive the buyers placing the manufacturers seal and logo id on these to make them appear to be real and not fake.

Usually the counterfeit artist needs to put a veneer or a thin plate of real precious metal on the top surface to give the coin the appearance of being real.
It is very disappointing for the buyer and a great loss of investment when they discover they have been ripped off by these fakes.

There is a lesson here that I believe we can learn to help us advance in our faith by observing these practices and corruption in the precious metal markets as I am seeing a picture forming into a prophetic message as follows.

This is what I believe the Lord is saying; *He wants to bring great discernment to know the genuine from the counterfeits and also, bring a removal of the mixture of impurities from the genuine faith by refinement and purification fires.*

He wants to replace the superficial veneer that has an appearance of good with the genuine and pure which is "Christ in you the hope of glory" reality that will transform believers to glow and radiate the glory that He purposes to pour out in this season, to renew, to restore, to revive what is dead into a resurrection life army of mountain moving faith warriors that demonstrate the Love Nature and Character of God, validated with signs and wonders.

"I AM raising up the genuine faith that I have purposed My people to have by the gift of Righteousness and the Grace abundantly provided, empowering believers to rise up in My power and strength in this day. Even in these turbulent times of change and shakings amongst the dark forces of chaotic confusion and corruption; there is no match for My blood bought victory for mankind.
Let My will be done on earth as it is in Heaven. My Kingdom come as you offer yourselves as living sacrifices, upskilling to a renewed mind that no longer conforms to the patterns of this world, but is inspired by the Holy Spirit of truth and power."

The gold and silver coins are usually weighed to compare the size with what should be the correct weight for gold and silver. Usually the fake are bigger in size to try to mimic the weight, as gold is particularly heavy in substance compared to other metals.

Note the desirable properties of gold; it does not tarnish, fade or rust like other metals, making it a very pure and sought after metal of great value.

The Father wants to impart the pure substance of Heaven to His Special Peculiar People, to be containers of the great glory of His presence and not be puffed up with fake pride and self righteous religious practices, that only carry a superficial appearance of what is good.

He also does not want mixtures of man made false doctrines, that deny the power of the cross and the blood of Jesus for Salvation and also the false teaching that allows corrupt mixtures of impurities, to invade what is truth, disabling the genuine faith of God.

2 Corinthians 4:7
7 But we have this treasure in earthen vessels, that the excellence of the power may be of God and not of us

Know that the enemy would delight to keep us bound and ineffective with mixtures and impurities, living defeated by shame and guilt and remaining unrefined vessels, full of dross, with carnal besetting habits that hinder our effective witness as His representatives. There is coming a time of purification and refinement with the testing of our faith, which will result in genuine advancement to His Kingdom come on earth, through the equipping of a Mighty Army of believers who carry the Glory of God wherever their feet shall tread.

Just as the fake coins are copied from an imperfect die and cast with revealing signs that something just isn't quite right. Know this in your knower, "I have given an anointing that teaches all these things, My sheep know my voice and don't follow the voice of a stranger."

Chapter 4

Knowing

Discernment is available with eyes to see and ears to hear and it comes from a willingness to offer ourselves as His chosen vessels and as we allow the refinement process of the Lord to work through us like the baptism of fire igniting our hearts; our minds will be heightened with uncompromised insight; we will be able to see the hidden agendas that have held us captive and finally break free.

Discernment develops, as we put into practice what we have received, knowing the difference between good and evil. *Heb 5:14*
Counterfeits, Lies, Deceptions.
Conspiracies, cunning plots and schemes, the wiles of the enemy.
Infiltrations by agents of darkness into churches, doctrines mingled with lies to blind believers to lies.

In the end times deceivers will increase, false Christs, false prophets, false teachers, false brethren, these may even deceive the elect.

Troubling times indeed, if we don't lean on the Lord for understanding, in our own intellect we will, be blindsided, taken for a smooth ride by the operators who appear to be in the light. Takes a keen eye to pick it, those counterfeiters are clever and go to great lengths to make something appear legitimate.

The trained eye will pick it up and with much use, get better and will feel the differences.

Trust the still small voice, the nudges, the promptings, an impression, the feelings of discord, a clanging, a bad taste, however you pick up things go with it, ask the Holy Spirit for clarity and what to do with the information, He will lead you into all truth and show you things to come.

As we come into agreement with the Word of God, which is like a Sword, dividing the motivations of the heart, the soul and mind, impurities are removed, what were blockages to doing the right thing will be realigned to His love and purposes.

We therefore, need to persevere in the trials when the heat is turned up beyond the comfort zone, continue in His purposes to be found in the purity of gold.

With clarity of mind, we can put into practice wisdom from above and locate the paths to victory and we may also, liberate others from the strongholds that keep us restrained, in the cunning plans and deceptions of the enemy.

Discernment is required to detect the operations of the agents of darkness, we will also perceive the ministers of light, which are heavens angels, they are sent to assist us and by seeing them, sensing them, we can cooperative with the directives of Heaven.

"Remember I AM a discerner of hearts and I know what is in man and you have now been given what is mine by the Holy Spirit who lives in you and reveals things to you."

This is a call to be totally dependent on Him to know truth as many false ministers with lying signs and wonders are released and will be released in the future to counter the genuine, this is always the plan of the enemy to steal, kill and destroy our eternal life in Christ Jesus by deception, that is his nature and what he does.

Philippians 1:9-11 New King James Version (NKJV)
9 And this I pray, that your love may abound still more and more in knowledge and all discernment,
10 that you may approve the things that are excellent, that you may be sincere and without offense till the day of Christ,
11 being filled with the fruits of righteousness which are by Jesus Christ, to the glory and praise of God.

I don't feel that the Lord is saying we have failed here, but rather it is a call, a challenge, an opportunity to grow and learn from our mistakes and shortcomings, His desire is for us to come up higher with Him and Rule and Reign in this life.

This is His intention from what He purchased for us, by suffering in our place on the cross to make us overcomers in this life. We are co-heirs with Jesus as we also suffer with Him by losing our life to gain true life.

Remember His kindness leads us to repentance, so let's change our ways and thinking and receive His invite to come up where He is and then share with those he brings into our lives, what He has freely given to us.

As the darkness gets darker, the light will become brighter, we must not be in fear, Jesus said His peace He has given to us and He has overcome the world.

So this day rise up in the strength and authority that He has commissioned you with,
be Agents of change in this day and age.

Chapter 5

The Game Changers

The Throne of Iniquity is like the Game of the Thrones of Iniquity.
There is an actual Game called Life, it has rules and pathways to follow which involves choice.
But, our life is not a game and is not really played for fun, it is for real.
There is opposition to stop you from getting to the place you aspire to be.
These powers that mastermind schemes using the power of iniquity are ruling from thrones hidden in darkness, what we need to understand is that when you are on a conquest to succeed in life, how the enemy operates to undermine your advancement?
Another aspect to iniquity is described as the Mystery of Iniquity in the Word of God, revealing the complexity and the subtle nature of the strategies used by these dark powers to influence the subjects; that's us men and women on the journey of life.

Just to help the reader understand here is my interpretation of the word iniquity and how it is applied in this book.
"Iniquity is the patterns of behaviour that are laid on the tracks of our minds, creating a permanent memory bias, when triggered by certain events in life, will influence us to make wrong choices. Iniquity allows sin or wrong choices to take root and set up a dominion within your soul."

Within the powers and influence of Iniquity there will be the following effects on mankind:

Opposition to those who have faith in God and have committed their life to the Kingdom of God.

Offering alternative religious practices to following the true faith in God.

Another way that is counterfeit Christianity or a false religion that may also have counterfeit signs and wonders.

Distorted interpretations of the Word of God to create the Doctrines of Men.

Accusations where you have missed the mark in the law used to condemn you.

Legal Ground to attack your life through iniquity.

Patterns of the Past.

The Throne of Iniquity has the legal right to rule over those that are under its sway and influence.

Iniquity has an access to the point of entry to sway your thinking, pull you down and drive you to destruction.

Driven behaviour is overwhelming and has a lot of momentum and push power to drive you in a wrong direction like an out of control freight train, you have seen those movies, very difficult to contain.

Addictions and lust are driving forces that push you into paths of destruction.

Iniquity will shut you down, kills the vibrancy of the personality from the weight of its rule and domination. The result brings a crippled inside, due to oppression and out of control emotions. Joy and healthy expression has been stolen.

Psalm 94:20
20 Shall the throne of iniquity which devises evil by LAW
Have fellowship with you?

How do these devious creatures from the hideous throne of iniquity have access into our lives?
Well through the tool of iniquity, a sinful lifestyle and mindset that brings us down to their level.
Why?
Because the law brings judgment and removes us from the benefits of God.
So here is the question do they have fellowship with you? What is it like?
By being like minded and having the same kind of heart in darkness that is separate to God's love, having a focus on the lust for things and power.

No opposing might or power can stop the church from fulfilling its mandate to be Christ in us and His will done on earth as it is heaven from an endless life of abundance of grace to the church; who are ruling and reigning with Christ in the Heavenly Realms far above all other principalities and the dominions of darkness and the effects of iniquity in the hearts of men.
(Taken from the book called "Grace Be Grace Do" by the same author)

Iniquity is Entrenched in Layers.
The Mystery is not easily identified and becomes a Complex Labyrinth for those who go down the long dark tunnels deep into the endless rabbit hole, no end in sight.

This requires a lot of investigation to reveal, as there is a lot going on beneath the surface.

Ephesians 4:14
¹⁴ that we should no longer be children, tossed to and fro and carried about with every wind of doctrine, by the trickery of men, in the cunning craftiness of deceitful plotting,
This is evidence of cunning schemes and agendas of mankind.
Now you need to know that the Powers that rule in the alternative realms of the multi-verse need men and women to operate through, theses are their instruments that do their bidding and are given authority influence fame and fortune or whatever they need to be cooperative.
Ephesians 6:12
¹² For we do not wrestle against flesh and blood, but against principalities, against powers, against the rulers of the darkness of this age, against spiritual hosts of wickedness in the heavenly places.

The system or philosophy developed as an alternative to being submitted to God our creator, says that we can be independent and so called free.
It must be cleverly disguised to deceive and offer rewards to entice.
Convince us that God is doing us harm.

The power and strength of iniquity:
Alluring
Glitters
Charms
Ability to deceive by the fruit that is offered like the original sin
Dark knowledge
Puffs up
Arrogant
False Humility

Counterfeit
Appears to be in the light
Superior to the uninformed
Calls right wrong, above the law
Own Religion Own Rules
Promised Freedom from Authority
Free Agent
Independence, make your own rules
Holds those captive enslaved by its entwining intermingling deceptive power.
A snake coiled about victims wraps them in its thinking
Blindness to the truth
You cant see that you are in pride.

Thrones can be compared to the Mountains of the World.
Places and fields of influence.
Empowering, like something given, like a false grace to its chosen subjects, to help control and influence the masses under its sway.
Believers rise up and take your place, may the will of God be done on earth as it is in Heaven, His Kingdom come.
We can speak grace, grace to the mountain!!!
(Zechariah)
We have been given Authority as Kings and Priests to rule and reign in Christ Jesus.
We are His representatives and His voice on earth to make a difference.
What mountain of influence are you directed to minister to?
There is a reaction going on, similar to cause and effect and this is the effect on the trends and mindset of the times effecting a region, or a whole nation going into the whole world.

When God's law was introduced, the purpose was so mankind could plainly see that all have missed the mark and need to change their ways to meet a proper standard, this leads us to the Good News, all need a Saviour and so Jesus Christ was sent to save mankind. *God so loved the world, that He sent his only Son not to condemn mankind but to save all (John 3)*, that means everyone who is believes and receives can be saved.

In the worlds system in Government, the governing rulers over people will also require laws to maintain order. However, as it goes when you put mankind in charge, laws which were originally intended for good may also be used as a system of control, to enslave those under in an unjust rule, this may eventually lead to civil unrest, then an uprising occurs from the reactions of the unjust use of laws and penalties to the oppressed masses.

What follows is a reactionary movement which can affect a whole nation and then have a world wide influence, changing the fabric of society. The pendulum will then swing to the opposite end.

Think of the revolutions that have over thrown dictatorships, shifts in the 1960's away from hard line, authoritarian rule resulting in wars to freedom to slaves, racism challenged moving into times of peace and hippy love, singing the anthems of freedom. This applies usually to democratic countries in the West, but history has proven that even oppressive dictatorships can crumble from uprisings. I see that the pendulum in the West particularly has swung to where the structures and the walls that have oppressed free expression have been torn down and we have formed a liberal state, where tolerance and no absolutes may sway justice and the standards of the perfect law.

Now if you question the reasoning of the Free State, you maybe met with a swinging and sometimes irrational, reaction including violence.

Why would they reject sound advice? Because of the embedded memories from the wounds, hurts, traumas, by the injustice from harsh authorities, the failings of religious institutions and individuals that have transgressed and caused harm to others.
This is a strong emotion and it will over ride reasoning things out over a cuppa, discussing both points of view, arriving at a resolution that benefits all.

Getting back to the holy prophet of God Isaiah, who cried out *"woe is me, a man of iniquity and unclean lips"*, where does it leave us who are the masses, we who barely know God if at all?

Do you see now the need for all to walk the hot coals walk, before we can talk the talk? Enter into the refinement by the baptism of fire, which purifies our improper distortions that are set deep into our thinking, emotions and memories, going off like fire crackers when the flame touches us.
What is the true state of freedom?

God's idea of freedom is being set free from the power and effects of sin, where the destructive consequences of sin no longer have dominion or rule over us.
The word sin, can have a lot of emotive connotations in our language and the psyche of a liberal thinking person, wanting freedom from the perceived shackles of harsh and judgmental religion. God is viewed as the harsh judge sitting way above and wanting to punish everyone who gets it wrong.

A bit like the Headmaster with a huge stick, who has a gleam on his face as he administers the blows to the rebels in the classroom. Well that's how it was in the bad old days, when physical punishment was the norm for offenders. We really are the swingers, like those balls on the pendulum bumping and bashing one direction or another never finding an equilibrium or rest.

Who can blame us from rebelling and wanting out from the harsh dictator? But what about when we have done wrong and there is consequences due?

Sin actually means missing the mark. So, all have sinned and missed the mark, no one is exempt and we all need a Saviour.

There is no possible utopia, we have tried the commune and freedom colonies with the best intentions and they all inevitably become corrupted even with a so called freedom for all philosophy, Why, because all have missed the mark and will inevitably sin.

No laws, no restraints, apparently free from the system. Freedom from the system of a dictator is a good thing. I enjoy the freedoms and liberties of the West, I would rather have those than be under a harsh dictator, Nero, Hitler and plenty more examples from history litter our evolution. Put man in charge without God and you will have extremes, without the truth in love and true justice administered in pure wisdom.

Most would agree that we do need some laws, to stop anarchy; nobody wants looters, thieves, to rob their place and not have a police force to stop them.

Even in the famed Wild West there was some sort of order by the appointed Sheriffs and Deputies, even if they were corrupt they maintained some semblance of civil order to protect the community.

We need to wake up to something, God put us in charge of the place, we rebelled against His oversight, we allowed a shifting of the balance of the law, who then is the Authority? Whoever gets to be in charge! That's why we need to pray for those in Government, so that they would come into the Light, adjust their ways, remove the influences of imbalanced dark agendas.

Without God, we remove one system only to have another system take its place with a skewed set of extremes and a contrived justice system that is biased; the wisdom of man is foolishness.

Proverbs 8:13 - 17
[13] The fear of the Lord is to hate evil;
Pride and arrogance and the evil way
And the perverse mouth I hate.
[14] Counsel is mine, and sound wisdom;
I am understanding, I have strength.
[15] By me kings reign,
And rulers decree justice.
[16] By me princes rule, and nobles,
All the judges of the earth.
[17] I love those who love me,
And those who seek me diligently will find me.

Be in the Light as He is in the Light.

If the Son sets you free you are free indeed.

Chapter 6

Write New Tracks for your Life

Negative self talk
Chatter that sends us into a spiral
Is an enemy of our thinking, emotional stability and physical well being.

We can be under attack by forces, which are something like malicious programs that infiltrate our thinking and corrupt our operating system.
The malicious code usually comes in by stealth, embeds into our thinking, appearing to be part of our normal thinking processes and disguising itself to look like our normal system.
Entwined into our thoughts, emotions and memories over time, gradually building up into being integrated into our DNA, this can lead us to believe that is just who we are, it is part of our identity.
Usually the malicious thoughts enter us when we are most vulnerable most often in the time of our youth, this is when our defenses are undeveloped and we are not able to properly discern what is happening, we all go through traumas and shocking experiences, but as a young person these are harder to deal with and resist.

We need to recognize that the negative self talk is at work inside us and we have accepted the adverse chattering in our minds which has influenced our moods, emotions, behaviours that robs our lives of our best potential.

Even if we don't know what caused it, or it wasn't our fault, we need to take action to disarm these toxic thoughts and reset our pathway to victory.
Then we must set up a defense system, and replace all negative talk with the truth about who we really are and can be.

There is hope for our future.
Because we are loved and accepted by God our Heavenly Father, Family and Friends.
They know our potential and accept us where and are, encouraging us to take steps to wholeness because nothing is too hard for God.
Our True Identity is who God created us to be, a wonderful unique expression.

True and correct thoughts will eventually rewrite the tracks in our brain, memories and will not trigger the harmful emotions that send us into a downward spiral.
The healing process and thinking reset leads us to good health, physical well being as the bodys defense systems are not overloaded and fighting constantly in the resistance to attack.

Antidote…….
Be Thankful.
Be kind to others and yourself seeing the best in them.
Don't be anxious ask God for help and allow Him to take charge.
Philippians 4: 7 "and the peace of God, which surpasses all understanding, will guard your hearts and minds through Christ Jesus."

Think on good things, occupy your mind with uplifting and peaceful thoughts.

Remember the blood of Jesus cleanses us from all past mistakes, failings and removes all shame and guilt.
No one is perfect we all got our stuff to deal with.

Next you need to go to the root cause of each individual toxic thought, which become lies when we accept them or allow them to control our lives.

Try to remember when these thoughts first came and what triggered them?
Ask God the Holy Spirit to lead you and show you each one and the source of it so then you can deal with it.
Renounce it – make a choice, an act of your will, change your mind
Restrain it from having influence on your life – in the Name of Jesus
Be released from the effects of it. – in the Name of Jesus
Remember, God is greater than anything this life throws at us and you will need to trust Him and depend on His power to do this. Grace is ability given from above.
You may need help to identify these from a Counsellor/Minister, who is experienced to deal with this.

Also, some deeply rooted negative influences in our thinking may be very resistant and you will need help to remove these.

Some habit patterns are very ingrained and will take time to completely change, so you need to persist and repeat until you see permanent change.

Things that took years to effect us take time to work through. But you can expect to have some very positive breakthroughs that will transform your life.

Remember the butterfly effect.
Metamorphosis is transformation, takes time for the caterpillar to go to chrysalis and then fight its way out of the cocoon, butterfly DNA completely changed.
All things are possible, only believe.

Write New Tracks for your Life like the *CD Writer*, God's Glory Light is brighter and stronger than any contamination and can restore the tracks to a healthy harmonious sound.

Remember the enemy is called the Accuser of the Brethren, that's what he does.
It is in his nature and his operation to wear us down and keep us subdued.

The enemy will bring to our mind in amplified fashion, emphasising all of our failings and how much we break highlighted laws, if you don't resist him he will gain a stronghold in your mind to take you out of the picture.

Yes, when we do wrong, we do need to make it right, but it is by the Fathers guiding hand, leading us to change our lifestyle to be on the right tracks.
Isaiah knew he was a man of iniquity and he had lips that have spoken the wrong things, coming into agreement with the dark whisperings.
There is a battle going on in our heads and it can take us out and into a severe depression, if we allow it to continue.

The hot coals can be intense, it may feel like burning, but in the end we will be much lighter, by the removal of toxic mindsets that were destroying our souls.

Some change takes time to develop, your Father is patient with us and His mercies are new every morning.

We need to start each day afresh on the right train of thought, guided to the track that has the light shining the way, peace leading us by our loving Heavenly Father who wants to spend eternity with us.

"Turn your eyes on Jesus and the things of this world will go strangely dim in the Light of His Glory and Grace." Traditional Gospel Song Adaption.

Chapter 7

In the Light

I am the Light of the world.
Go and sin no more.
John 8.

Here is two statements placed together, but when you first look at these next to each other you would not connect them at all, they seem to be two separate statements with no relation to each other.

They could be completely meaningless statements to some, but to those who have made the connection have been switched on to the connection and their light shines. These two statements are aligned and connected where one will activate the next.

Here is a question to be pondered, why did Jesus come to earth?
He is the light that lights up every man and woman. We know that He is the Saviour of Mankind,
He is the Way the Truth and the Life. John 14.
We now have access through Him and become part of the Family of Father God.

The Lord your God is offering this relationship to you through the finished work of Jesus.
That is where these statements become connected, through relationship and accepting the connection to the Father of our spirits.

Like a light turned on by electricity, it needs to be plugged in and connected and then switched on to work and show brilliance.
Sin is pretty much the disconnection to God, or separation from the way and the truth and the life, Jesus came since God so loved the world to make the connection for us to be part of the life flow from above.
Jesus came to destroy the works of the enemy and the power of sin and death.
We can now overcome by the faith of the Son of God.
This is the invitation to all by Him to receive the Life that is full of His Light.

Let him or her who has not sinned cast the first stone.
The woman caught in adultery was guilty for sure and according to the law punishable by death.
But Jesus didn't come to condemn mankind but rather to save them.
We all fall short of the Glory of God, maybe not in the same way as this woman who committed a more obvious act, but there is always something in our makeup where we give into the nature of sin and enter rebellion from God.
Stubbornness is like the sin of witchcraft, which is rebellion and lawlessness.
How is the tongue? Ever spoken evil words against someone or even yourself?
We can either bless or curse by the power of the tongue and those words have effect for darkness on the negative or to be light giving on the positive.
Noone who is honest and has allowed the Light of the world to reveal the darkness within is going to cast a stone at another.
This is condemning someone to death which is sending them to their eternal destruction.

God loves mercy not judgement.
Judgement will come into effect for those who have refused Gods mercy as a lifetime choice, unless they repent and change their lifetime choices by receiving His Light in His mercy towards us.

There is a light shining in the darkness.
When we invite His Light to shine this will fill the darkness and change the properties to pure light energy, which changes the motivations of darkness to be light.
Go and sin no more is possible when we go through this metamorphosis like the butterfly, changed to be free to fly and become a beautiful, colourful new creation.

God knows our potential and who He created us to be and how we are wonderfully made to be, when we allow His light to shine into our hearts and minds made up of emotions, our will, memories and reasoning for our life choices and decisions, our life becomes just like the butterfly coming out from the chrysalis, transformed from the crawling, devouring, ground dweller into a magnificent new creation, and this is how God sees us and who He created us to be.

When Jesus saw the woman caught in adultery, that is how He saw her as the new creation butterfly, no longer bound by the old behaviours of the past, so He opened the way for her to receive the Light of His Brilliant Person to activate the change in her life.
He then said the statement of transformation, *"go and sin no more"* this is our new lifestyle, because Jesus is *"I am the Light of the world"* and this Light will give you the ability to enter into the miraculous metamorphosis like the butterfly.

We are set free from bondages of this earth and released from the patterns of behaviour and the mindset that keeps you there.

This Light is shining now and all who receive it will be partakers of the divine nature in the person and image of Jesus.

There is a song that *DC Talk* performed, which was written by *Charlie Peacock* who also performed the song, "Be in the Light".

Some of the lyrics are,
*"I want to be in the Light as He is in the Light
I want to shine like the stars in Heaven."*

Appropriate words, worth listening to and receiving the message.

I believe the Father desires to have believers that will shine His reflection in a radiant brilliance into the world, and wherever His Light goes in His people, brings illumination of the way, the truth and the life in ever increasing measures, releasing millions in this end time harvest to be turned on, switched on and light up their lives.

God has a three phase plan to plug us into some ultra high voltage increases, so we will be connected to the generator of His Divine Power connections.

The Light that lights up every man is getting brighter, even as the darkness gets darker the more intense the true light shines.

The greater works of Jesus are released by the Glory Light Carriers, these are the coming manifested sons and daughters of the Most High God and nothing will be able to resist this intensity of Light in its brightness; all that has dark properties and counterfeit light comes from the dark forces and will be expelled, ushering in freedom to the captives within the domains, communities, regions and where ever the Glory is sent.

Chapter 8

Take the Joshua Challenge

Joshua was an old man, but he was commissioned to lead the Nation of Israel across the Jordan River into the Promised Land.
The promised land was bountiful and was not a desert, but a beautiful place full of goodness and abundant blessings.

However, giants and strange people possessed the land that served idols and had fierce gods ruling over them.
Joshua had the Word of God and the promises to move him from a wandering in the desert mentality and the slavery thinking of the past that dominated the nation of Israel generationally.

Joshua 1
3 Every place that the sole of your foot will tread upon I have given you, as I said to Moses.
4 From the wilderness and this Lebanon as far as the great river, the River Euphrates, all the land of the Hittites, and to the Great Sea toward the going down of the sun, shall be your territory.
5 No man shall be able to stand before you all the days of your life; as I was with Moses, so I will be with you. I will not leave you nor forsake you.
6 Be strong and of good courage, for to this people you shall divide as an inheritance the land which I swore to their fathers to give them.

7 Only be strong and very courageous, that you may observe to do according to all the law which Moses My servant commanded you; do not turn from it to the right hand or to the left, that you may prosper wherever you go.
8 This Book of the Law shall not depart from your mouth, but you shall meditate in it day and night, that you may observe to do according to all that is written in it. For then you will make your way prosperous, and then you will have good success.
9 Have I not commanded you? Be strong and of good courage; do not be afraid, nor be dismayed, for the Lord your God is with you wherever you go."

Meditation and speaking the word and the promises was the instruction for Joshua and the Nation of Israel.
Why would they need to do this?
They couldn't see themselves as more than conquerors and able to defeat the very powerful opposition in the strongholds and fierce armies of the Canaanites that possessed the place that God has promised to His chosen people, this is a place of prosperity in the land flowing with milk and honey.

Meditation is planting and feeding on the Word of God to transform our thinking, so that we will rise up and take possession of what belongs to us.

This is a process of continued absorption of the Word of God into our consciousness, taking hold of the personal prophesies and promises of God, reminding us who we really are, which reconstructs how we see ourselves to have a vision of who God says we are.

Think back to the poor ugly caterpillar creature, crawling and creeping around on the leafy plants, all it did was devour, eat the goodness and nutrients of leaves as it moved along the path of survival.

Job 22
28 You will also declare a thing,
And it will be established for you;
So light will shine on your ways.

Decree and Declare is how we establish the thing and the thing is what He has said our life will be.
What are we doing to establish in our lives what God has said will be and who we will be?
This is coming into agreement with God and not being led by fear, doubt and unbelief and what the circumstances or our past or what others have said will be, we will no longer accept what is contrary to what God has promised to us, to have and to be and to do.
When we come into agreement with God, we are activating who we are and what He has promised into our lives and this is a faith walk across the hot coals and into the Promised Land.

This is tearing down fortresses and scattering strange gods that oppose us from having our inheritance, which rightfully belongs to the children of God.
The light of life will shine on our ways and that is a real good thing.

Philippians 4:5-8 New King James Version (NKJV)
5 Let your gentleness be known to all men. The Lord is at hand.
6 Be anxious for nothing, but in everything by prayer and supplication, with thanksgiving, let your requests be made known to God;

7 and the peace of God, which surpasses all understanding, will guard your hearts and minds through Christ Jesus.
8 Finally, brethren, whatsoever things are true, whatsoever things are honest, whatsoever things are just, whatsoever things are pure, whatsoever things are lovely, whatsoever things are of good report; if there be any virtue, and if there be any praise, think on these things.

We have an attitude of expectation and trust in our God and we are thankful for what He has given us and what He has prepared for our future as our provider and deliverer.

Philippians 2
12 Therefore, my beloved, as you have always obeyed, not as in my presence only, but now much more in my absence, work out your own salvation with fear and trembling;
13 for it is God who works in you both to will and to do for His good pleasure.
14 Do all things without complaining and disputing,
15 that you may become blameless and harmless, children of God without fault in the midst of a crooked and perverse generation, among whom you shine as lights in the world,
16 holding fast the word of life, so that I may rejoice in the day of Christ that I have not run in vain or labored in vain.

This is working out our salvation in order that we see the blessings and the benefits come into our lives, as we serve God and are obedient to His leading and surrender our agendas into His will be done on earth as it is in Heaven.

We don't get to shine like lights unless we allow the light to inhabit and remove our darkness and lighting up all of the dark places in our souls.

Hebrews 3
7 Therefore, as the Holy Spirit says:
"Today, if you will hear His voice,
8 Do not harden your hearts as in the rebellion,
In the day of trial in the wilderness,
9 Where your fathers tested Me, tried Me,
And saw My works forty years.
10 Therefore I was angry with that generation,
And said, 'They always go astray in their heart,
And they have not known My ways.'
11 So I swore in My wrath,
'They shall not enter My rest.'"
12 Beware, brethren, lest there be in any of you an evil heart of unbelief in departing from the living God;
13 but exhort one another daily, while it is called "Today," lest any of you be hardened through the deceitfulness of sin.
14 For we have become partakers of Christ if we hold the beginning of our confidence steadfast to the end,
15 while it is said:
"Today, if you will hear His voice,
Do not harden your hearts as in the rebellion."
16 For who, having heard, rebelled? Indeed, was it not all who came out of Egypt, led by Moses?
17 Now with whom was He angry forty years? Was it not with those who sinned, whose corpses fell in the wilderness?
18 And to whom did He swear that they would not enter His rest, but to those who did not obey?
19 So we see that they could not enter in because of unbelief.

We don't want to be scattered in the desert without reaching our promised land due to Unbelief, Fear and Doubt, the enemies of our soul.
The Israelites had bad speech issues, which contaminated their minds, resulting in hard and rebellious hearts, which kept them from receiving the promises and an abundant inheritance.

It is important that we humble ourselves under His mighty hand and allow His leading through the process of refinement which perfects our faith, which develops a purified heart that we may enter into the promises of God for our lives.

Praying in the spirit was a practice that was instructed to believers to not lose the faith and build themselves up in faith, to be overcomers. *Jude 20.*
Dave Roberson's Book *"The Walk in the Spirit the Walk of Power"* is excellent teaching on the walk of faith mentioned, the walk of victory.
Speaking in tongues is the pure language like pure gold it flows and is has no impurities mixed in.

Take the Joshua challenge, for young or old, this is your life, this is your victory.
Just as the caterpillar needs the time of preparation to form into the freedom of the butterfly, so do we need to eat the nutrition of the word.
The caterpillar didn't suddenly transpose from being a caterpillar to a butterfly, no it first of all intuitively formed a chrysalis wall of protection to encase the birthing process. During these delicate stages the caterpillar needed to enter into rest and be still, while the development took place without disrupting the flow.

This takes precious time to be ready for a break out of the old shell and it involved strengthening unused muscles and the newly developed limbs and now wings in order to be able to fly and become this newly formed magnificent creature, a wonder to behold.

These are all the enhanced gifts, talents and abilities from above, that we receive when we are empowered by the Spirit of God for service and advancing the Kingdom of God on earth. We are new creatures who demonstrate love with signs and wonders revealed to those who are needy and they know that the message of God is true.

We are learning to fly into the promises, the exploits, in the elevations of the new perspectives of the wonders of God, we are soaring in harmony by the anointing of the Holy Spirit.

Chapter 9

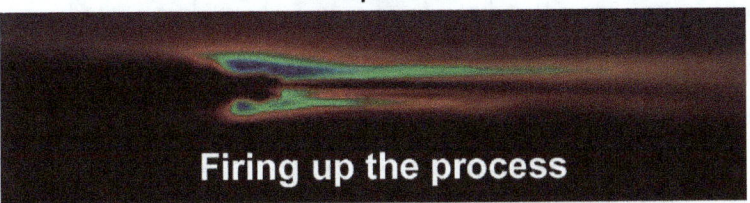

Firing up the process

Hebrews 12
Therefore we also, since we are surrounded by so great a cloud of witnesses, let us lay aside every weight, and the sin which so easily ensnares us, and let us run with endurance the race that is set before us,
2 looking unto Jesus, the author and finisher of our faith, who for the joy that was set before Him endured the cross, despising the shame, and has sat down at the right hand of the throne of God.

Some may experience a real challenge to overcome and lay aside their pet sins.

Others have certain besetting sins that linger on and are deeply embedded into the psyche. All it takes is that trigger point and bingo back into the snare of the fowler.

The fowler knows how to snare his prey with some juicy irresistible bait.

"Goody goody", says the id when offered the bait, our id is the part of our identity that Freud has proposed, that just has to get what it wants at all costs.

"O wretched man that I am", says Paul in *Romans 7* as he describes the battle in his soul, I do what I do not want to do and still agree with the commandments of God that they are best for me.

Does this sound familiar, at any cost, we push aside the thought about consequences for our rash actions and proceed anyway down the dark alley of degradation?

Are we psychos on the loose, unrestrained, bent on destruction?
God help us! Save us all!
You know, God did help us and gave us a way out.

Easy? No!

You have heard of the narrow path and then the broad highway that sucks you downwards into the spiral of defeat.
We need to focus on the end game. Keep our eternal destination in our sights and we shall go through the challenges and temptations into a better person.
What a friend we have in Jesus, He is walking it out with us on this journey of faith, He is at the beginning of our faith and He continues to walk and talk us through to the finish line.

Endurance, we need endurance to continue and allow His workings in our life to purge out the dross, which is excess baggage that keeps us earth bound to the bad habits we have picked up in this world.

Consider the concept that iniquity cannot co-exist with the perfection of God and imperfections cannot stand in the everlasting Kingdom, where our earthly bodies will be transformed by the resurrection process of perfecting our corrupted earthly beings.
Isaiah got a taste of this fiery process when the hot coal touched his lips.
Particularly, what came out of his mouth was refined.
He was a man of unclean lips
He could then stand with new found confidence in the presence of God, once the iniquity was removed.
God is asking *"Whom shall I send, and who will go for us?"*

Out of Isaiah's mouth came *"here am I; send me"*.
As a man thinks, so is he, the intentions and motivations of our inner most beings is exposed and tested and cannot endure the brightness of the purity of God.

What is all this fire and burning for, really, is it just a kill joy?

No consider this, preparation for eternity and a new life where the old has passed away.
The question is who will be sent? Who will go? Will there be end time prophets, spokesmen and spokeswomen of God, who have gone through the refining process to be cleansed and prepared for the master's use?

How then shall we live in these end times harvest of lost souls, where there is an enormous need to deliver mankind from destruction, before we completely annihilate the planet? How can we prepare ourselves and confidently be the light shining in places of darkness? In other words do we have the goods?
Or are we just like everyone else, blending in with those around us who are struggling and just do life in survival mode?

What if we had a Heavenly encounter like Isaiah? We would be forever changed and make a difference in this world?

Having an encounter is personal and individual, we should not expect to have an experience exactly like Isaiah, because we are all different and God deals with each of us differently.

However, we do need to interact with God by faith, have an ongoing personal relationship with Him in order that the two way flow can occur, which means we will encounter Him as a lifestyle experience to a variety of degrees, bringing transformation, from glory to glory. This is how we should live in our challenging day and age and let God move in our lives in accordance with His purposes and plans for each of our lives.

No one is perfect that is correct, but someone who is being perfected by a worthy process, becoming as He is in this world would have something to offer to those who are drowning and pulled down stream by the raging currents of our times.

There is an Elijah generation coming into these times who will have their very DNA regenerated with fire, they will be known as having genuine character, the real thing, infinitely better than Coke and they will have a testimony, all shame and disgrace is removed, signs and wonders are following these ones who know God and who are strong and do mighty exploits.

Earth shakers are coming like earth quakes in various places, the status quo and what seems to be acceptable will be shaken to the core as the truth revealed pierces the shadows and corruption of the worldly manmade, belief systems.
What appears to be OK and meets the approval of those who seem to be something, on the surface may look good, but when the brilliance of the laser level is applied, all of the warped philosophies and crooked ways will be exposed.

Plastic is like a shiny veneer, plastic melts when the heat is turned up, it buckles and goes an ugly, sooty colour. All manmade superficial, situational ethics and so called acceptable practices, like plastic veneer that has being burnt and decayed, will be seen for what it is.

Hebrews 12:25-29
25 See that you do not refuse Him who speaks. For if they did not escape who refused Him who spoke on earth, much more shall we not escape if we turn away from Him who speaks from heaven,
26 whose voice then shook the earth; but now He has promised, saying, "Yet once more I shake not only the earth, but also heaven."
27 Now this, "Yet once more," indicates the removal of those things that are being shaken, as of things that are made, that the things which cannot be shaken may remain.
28 Therefore, since we are receiving a kingdom which cannot be shaken, let us have grace, by which we may serve God acceptably with reverence and godly fear.
29 For our God is a consuming fire.

What is the purpose of fire?
To remove impurities that degrade elements, to make something durable and perform to its design, it is getting rid of the junk that is in the way of what is good.

To remove things that can be shaken, the things in our souls that cannot stand up to the presence of God and exist in a perfect place in Heaven.

His voice shakes not only the earth where sin is rampart, but the heavens where rebellion exists in the realms of the multi layered universe and lower regions where fallen angels, corrupted creatures and monsters of legends roam, where vile and wandering evil spirits who inhabit bodies originate, this is Satan's domain and influence.

If on earth we cannot escape the scrutiny of God's weighing up of heart motives and the purity of our actions, how much more when we contact Heaven will the fire burn with intensity to purify our elements and thinking and whatever else is in our hearts that offends.

That is why it is so important to deal with our issues on the way, on our pathway of life to become mature and accept the disciplines of our Heavenly Father that purges our imperfections to make a better me and a better you, as long as we submit to His process.

Bear in mind that the Bible says, *"Cast all of your cares on the Lord for He cares for you"*. He has your best interests at heart, it is for our benefit that we undergo His refining process, yes it is painful for a short while, but producing everlasting results. Wouldn't you rather have your stuff dealt with now, rather that have it burnt up with intensity on the final day with much loss?

1 Corinthians 3:12-13 King James Version (KJV)
12 Now if any man build upon this foundation gold, silver, precious stones, wood, hay, stubble;
13 Every man's work shall be made manifest: for the day shall declare it, because it shall be revealed by fire; and the fire shall try every man's work of what sort it is.

John the Baptist was the greatest prophet and he spoke about Jesus as One who is greater and who baptises not only with washing of water but also with a purifying fire.

The New Testament promises provide a better covenant with Him that brings a greater Glory upon our human frailties, when this occurs, like a chemical reaction of opposites, there is going to be sparks and abrasive friction.
Thank God we are in a process to be refined like pure gold by His Holy Fire.

The old is passing away, this earth and the whole universe as precious as it is and is displayed by wonder and beauty, is however in a state of decay, this world and the whole universe has an expiry date. So shouldn't we look forward to a better state of being as well?
There is a Day of the Lord spoken about, this is where God sorts out the issues and makes a clean sweep, removing the contaminations and bringing order into how things were intended to be.
2 Peter 3:10 – 13
10 But the day of the Lord will come as a thief in the night, in which the heavens will pass away with a great noise, and the elements will melt with fervent heat; both the earth and the works that are in it will be burned up.
11 Therefore, since all these things will be dissolved, what manner of persons ought you to be in holy conduct and godliness,
12 looking for and hastening the coming of the day of God, because of which the heavens will be dissolved, being on fire, and the elements will melt with fervent heat?

13 Nevertheless we, according to His promise, look for new heavens and a new earth in which righteousness dwells.

Jesus is qualified to administer fire to our beings. He is before all things and through Him all was created, He can restore as He knows how things should be. It is like a classic old car that has degenerated into a rusty pile of metal and old oil, we need a makeover, full restoration by the master engineer, back to authentic and original components or better than new condition. Included in this engineering ingenuity are the latest rust inhibiters and oil treatments, to preserve the vehicle to endure time and decay and also display the original character.

It has been stated that all iniquity is dealt with in a day.

Turn up the heat.

Do you like BBQ?

The heat is on!

Chapter 10

Soul Lift

King David spoke to his soul.
Psalm 103

David commanded his soul to align with Gods blessing and benefits.
There is a battle going on and it is internal as well as external.
Fear is a strong emotion that paralyses action, it will try to convince us that God won't come through for us and we will be stuck in the cocoon forever, never coming out to fly and entering into the new creation being.
The thing is it robs us of our promised future and the blessings of our promised land.
We can speak to our emotions and order them to line up with what is written about us, we can make the crooked things in our thinking made straight.
He hasn't given us a spirit of fear 2 Timothy 2:7
The spirit He gives us is power and love and these overtake our emotions to be a positive and uplifting energy.

The hot coal treatment fires us up, as we receive grace to be able to see and hear and be in the Glory of God, unashamed, cleansed, purified and free to run into our destiny.
We are changed from Glory to Glory by the presence of God.
Draw near to God and He draws near to us.

We are lifted up into the higher ways.
Dross that remains and builds up is a faith inhibitor.
The impurities cleanser to be applied is the refining fire.
When we worship God in spirit and truth we set ourselves above in the place where He is and this brings peace to the emotions and our troubled minds, as our entire beings become subject to the spirit.

Remember the principle what you give out comes back to you pressed down shaken together. The law of sowing and reaping takes effect in our lives.
We must be the wise person that builds on a rock and not sinking sand, or we will never get off the ground and fly, crippled by fear and paralysis.

It is progressive and it is changing in intensity, the more you go, the more you grow.
The tongue is a powerful instrument, when harnessed and trained, it can move mountains and create a whole new realms of existence, quantum physics applied.
Iniquity, impure, unclean, corrupt, doubt, fear and unbelief in rebellion cannot remain when the hot coal from heaven enters our mouths.

Our Lord Jesus Christ is speaking to His Church, He is the Alpha and the Omega, what He began in our lives He will complete. He was and He now is and He will be.
He affects our past our present and our future.

There is fire in His eyes and when He speaks, a sharp penetrating sword comes to divide what is pure, from what is impure.

Listen to Jesus warning to the church at Laodicea who were neither hot nor cold, they were lukewarm, in mediocrity, they were rich and had need of nothing in their own eyes, but they were in a poor spiritual state, they could not see in themselves that they had corruption mixed into the precious seed planted within. Their faith was fading away and they could not see that they were going downhill fast.

Revelation 3:18 – 22
18 I counsel you to buy from Me gold refined in the fire, that you may be rich; and white garments, that you may be clothed, that the shame of your nakedness may not be revealed; and anoint your eyes with eye salve, that you may see.
19 As many as I love, I rebuke and chasten. Therefore be zealous and repent.
20 Behold, I stand at the door and knock. If anyone hears My voice and opens the door, I will come in to him and dine with him, and he with Me.
21 To him who overcomes I will grant to sit with Me on My throne, as I also overcame and sat down with My Father on His throne.
22 "He who has an ear, let him hear what the Spirit says to the churches."

When you hear Him, let Him into your life, then you will overcome.
There is Time.
We have been given time to create.
Time is restricted to a linear event, but we can redeem time.
There is time to discover who we are to be and do.

Good Energy is Divine Power, Life and Godliness achieved.

Bad Energy still empowers, but not the good things written about us.
Energy is the power to create, but it needs the right motivation to drive it on the right pathways.

Be empowered from a position of being.
Then do from this.

The Kingdom is already within, we do from this being.

Don't deny it, Apply it!
Walk the talk!

Acts 2:1-4
When the Day of Pentecost had fully come, they were all with one accord in one place.
2 And suddenly there came a sound from heaven, as of a rushing mighty wind, and it filled the whole house where they were sitting.
3 Then there appeared to them divided tongues, as of fire, and one sat upon each of them.
4 And they were all filled with the Holy Spirit and began to speak with other tongues, as the Spirit gave them utterance.
Hot coals cleanses unclean lips from iniquity.
Become cleansed from the bad effects of internal and external negative talk.

Be commissioned to talk the good talk.

Speak in alignment to the Word of God, Pray in the Spirit, be renewed in your mind, declare what He has shown you and commissioned you to establish in your sphere of influence.

Job 22:28 New King James Version (NKJV)
28 You will also declare a thing,
And it will be established for you;
So light will shine on your ways.

John 1:4
4 In him was life; and the life was the light of men.

His will be done on earth as it is in Heaven.
Amen!

Walk the Talk on Hot Coals

2025 Edition
ISBN: 978-1-0670654-0-9

Peter Koren
Copyright Feb 2017
Under previous title *"The Hot Coal Walk Talk"*

http://www.beinginthelight.com/

Front Cover artwork and internal images design by Peter Koren.

Unless otherwise indicated, Bible quotations are taken from New King James Version of the Bible.
Copyright © 1982 by Thomas Nelson, Inc.
Used by permission. All rights reserved.

Other Books by this Author:

Grace Be Grace Do
This is about the struggles we experience as believers and God's anticipation of our inability to overcome. We find that God has a solution to our problems; He hasn't left us in the lurch. God has it sorted with Grace to Be and Grace to Do. Find out how to get on board to be and do overcoming in this life, get this book.

Older Brother the Other
This is about two brothers who didn't get on, you know the story, brothers in conflict, goes all the way through history and into our so called, sophisticated, post modern times. One brother was the *Prodigal Son* and the *Other Brother*, well he is the other brother with a chip on the shoulder. There has to be a way for the Father to resolve these differences, there is and it is miraculous. Find out more get this book.

Seeing Beyond 2020 Vision
Take a look at what's happening behind the scenes and through the hype. When you find your position of influence seated with Christ in the Heavenly realms you will have renewed insight, like the eagles. There is some riddles to solve by telling the story in parables, which helps the reader connect with real life scenarios to become involved and become the change agent they are created to be, for such a time as this.

Hope you enjoyed *"Walk the Talk on Hot Coals"*, if you could leave me a review that would be greatly appreciated, spread the word. Thanks! Peter Koren Author

About the author: I began writing short articles on websites in the early 2000's and gradually the gift has developed after much editing and updating the message.

My background is not primarily writing as I am by natural talents an artist and love to work visually, so this has been quite a journey beginning with the articles and extending into *"Grace Be Grace Do"* which began as early inspiration for an article which flowed on to my first ebook ever, this was not expected at all. Since then two more books have emerged out of the works. The next book to come forth *was "Older Brother the Other"* My latest books are, *"Walk the Talk on Hot Coals"* and *"Seeing Beyond 2020 Vision".* The process works like this, I believe in inspiration imparted to write, as ideas and impressions come into my thoughts and then it is my part to be the scribe, writing it down as I receive it to the best of my ability.

My family heritage is mainly Slovakian with a mixture of ancestry from the Wends and the Prussians who migrated to Australia, a very interesting mix indeed.
I had a God encounter at a young age and this was the beginning of my own peculiar message.
Anyway it is best you just read the books and the articles I have published and make up your own mind what to do with it.

Connect with Me:
Facebook: PeterKoren Author Page
Articles :- http://www.beinginthelight.com/
Articles :- http://www.himessage.com/

■■

Walk the Talk on Hot Coals
2025 Edition
Available as

978-1-0670654-0-9	Walk the Talk on Hot Coals 2025 Edition PaperBack
978-1-0670654-1-6	Walk the Talk on Hot Coals 2025 Edition Kindle
978-1-0670654-2-3	Walk the Talk on Hot Coals 2025 Edition PDF
978-1-0670654-3-0	Walk the Talk on Hot Coals 2025 Edition EPUB

www.ingramcontent.com/pod-product-compliance
Lightning Source LLC
Chambersburg PA
CBHW050442010526
44118CB00013B/1650